THE LITTLE BROWN BAT weighs only a few ounces but, like most bats, it is feared and hated by many people. By following one female Little Brown Bat through the cycle of a year in her life, the author hopes to dispel these fears and encourage, instead, a curiosity and respect for these useful and interesting little mammals.

A Cycle of Seasons:
The Little Brown Bat

By Lucille Wood Trost

Young Scott Books

To Chuck

Printed in U.S.A. All Rights Reserved.
Text © 1971 by Lucille Trost.

Published by Young Scott Books,
a Division of Addison-Wesley Publishing Co., Inc.,
Reading, Massachusetts · 01867.

Library of Congress Catalog Card No. 76-141666
SBN: 201-09260-3

The Little Brown Bat is known to scientists by the name of *Myotis lucifugus*. It is only one of many other insect-eating bats found in the United States. The Big Brown Bat—*Eptesicus fuscus*—closely resembles it although there are differences both in behavior and physical form. The most obvious difference in appearance is that the Big Brown Bat is four and one-half inches in length while the Little Brown Bat is only about three and one-half inches. Both are beautiful, harmless, and fascinating creatures.

AUTUMN

High on a mountain above a small northwestern town there was a deserted mine. Its dark entrance was almost hidden among wild currant bushes, sage, and the deep green of juniper trees. In the early autumn morning, there came to this opening a Little Brown Bat. She was tired. Behind her with the night lay many miles of mountainous country over which she had flown to reach this place where she had wintered for the five years of her life.

With quick and erratic flight, she entered the tunnel. Only a short distance into the mine, it seemed totally dark, yet the small brown creature did not hesitate or slow her flight until she had traveled far along the cool passages away from the entrance. At last she came to an enlarged part of the cave. There was a strong musty smell and the squeaking sounds of many other bats. The female bat pitched head upward toward the ceiling and grasped on with her thumbs and toes. She shuffled about until at last she hung head downward with her leathery wings folded umbrella-like close to her side.

Time passed and the Little Brown Bat slept. For many months she would not need to awaken. She had fed upon the plentiful food of summer and fall. Each night she had eaten several times her own weight of insects, and her body had become plump and full. Throughout the long stretch of winter the Little Brown Bat would slowly use the extra fat.

As she hung sleeping in the chill dark air, a number of changes took place. Her body temperature fell until it was almost the same as that of the cold but non-freezing air of the cave. Her heartbeat slowed to about one-fortieth its normal rate (from 400 times a minute to about 10 times a minute), and her breathing fell to about one-tenth its normal speed (from 200 breaths to 23 breaths a minute). Because of this greatly slowed living, the extra food or fuel of her body would keep her alive until spring.

The Little Brown Bat had not moved, but she was no longer a small mouselike figure hanging alone.

During the late autumn days other bats had come to sleep beside her, and after a while she was only one small body among a hundred others that formed a brown furry blanket hanging from the ceiling. Occasionally, one or another of the tiny creatures barely awoke and shifted about within the mass. Those bats on the outside moved farther in while warmer animals took their places on the edge. In this way the bats shared and preserved body warmth without a greater need for food.

The long winter dark continued. Particles of moisture beaded up on the fur of the bats. Centipedes and spiders scurried about the rocks. Mosquitoes occasionally buzzed from the crannies to feed upon the exposed skin of wings and ears. A slight shaking of the earth caused a small mass of dirt to slip to the floor. None of these things disturbed the bats.

Beyond the entrance of the mine the snows were deep and drifted, and the air was very cold. Life was hard for the wild animals. The jackrabbits sat in white cold caves of ice and chewed upon the sappy twigs of rabbit bush. Mule deer stomped, stripped the bushes, and huddled together in thin shelters of trees. These problems were unknown to the Little

Brown Bat. The outside temperature might sink to twenty degrees below zero, but the coldest of weather or the worst of storms could not reach or change her sleeping place far within the mountain. It remained always several degrees above freezing. For many weeks more the Little Brown Bat would sleep the deep slumber of hibernation.

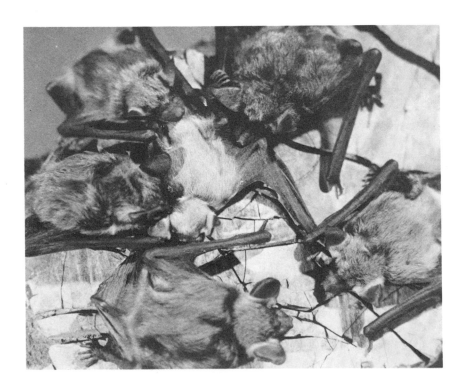

WINTER

One morning in January a man labored through the heavy snow and clear cold air to the mouth of the mine. He was a biologist—a scientist who studies the ways in which plants and animals live— and he had come to gather some information about the bats in the cave. Once within its entrance, he lit a miner's flashlight, which was fastened upon his head and allowed his hands to be free. With the strong white beam of light searching ceiling and walls, he continued along the old railroad tracks that led inward.

The first cluster of bats was a few minutes' walk from the entrance. Here the man paused briefly to look around, then continued deeper into the mine. At the next large group of bats he stopped and allowed his pack to slip from his back. Upon the cold earth floor he spread those things he would need for his work. There were a string of numbered aluminum bands, a notebook and pencil, a metal box with its attached long slender wire and temperature dials on the front (thermocouple), a ruler, and a stop watch.

The biologist stood first for a long while looking at the bats, then he began to walk about and to examine other things about the mine. He measured the temperature of the air and its moisture. He noted the number of bats and how they hung. He thrust up his hand and noticed that the outer surface of the cluster was cool and moist, but between the closely packed animals there was a very slight warmth. He shined the light close to the crusty white surfaces of the rock wall. Sow bugs scurried about like tiny tanks, while the mosquitoes loomed large in the shadows of the outcroppings. All of these things the man wrote into his notebook: the temperature was 34°F.; the humidity, 99%. The cluster of bats numbered about 100.

The Little Brown Bat suddenly felt herself plucked from her place on the ceiling. A hand held her by the loose skin on the back of her body. She squealed sharply and spread her wings. She opened her mouth to show the glimmer of her small sharp teeth. These

things made no difference to the biologist. He pushed the wire from the electric thermometer into her mouth and down her throat. After a short while the Little Brown Bat stopped struggling. It was hard to remain active when everything about her was slow and cold. Her temperature was 36°F., only two degrees higher than the slightly above-freezing air of the cave.

The man continued to hold and examine the Little Brown Bat. He stretched out her dark wings that

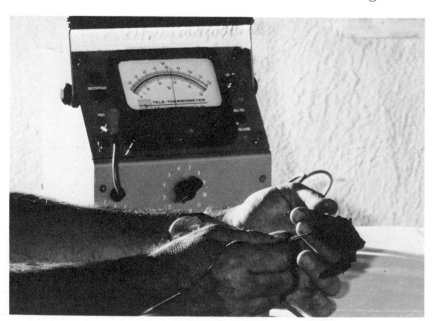

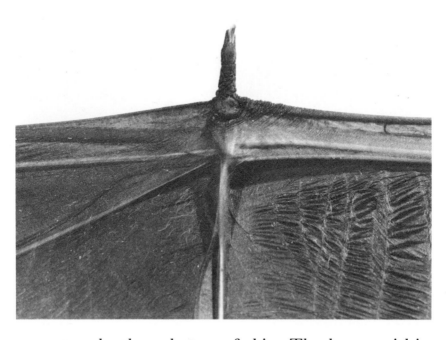

were two leathery layers of skin. The bones within
were very much like those of the arm and hand of
a man. There was a short upper-arm bone and below
that, a longer lower-arm bone. From these came four
very long slender finger bones which crossed the wing
like spokes. A tiny thumb bone with a sharp hooked
claw stuck up at the spot where the fingers left the
arm. There was a second leathery membrane between
her legs and tail. The man measured and recorded the
lengths of some of the bones. He examined the fur

in search of tiny animals—such as fleas or ticks—that might live upon her, but found none. He looked closely at her many small, sharp teeth. Finally the man placed a numbered silver band upon her leg.

Gradually, as the biologist held her, the breathing of the Little Brown Bat had become faster and faster. Once the awakening had begun, it could not stop until she was fully awake. Her heartbeat had grown much more rapid, and the temperature of her body increased by two degrees a minute. At last she began to shiver and made more frequent tries to escape from the gloved hand that held her fast. When her body temperature had reached 85°F., the Little Brown Bat again could fly.

When at last the man released her on a ledge of rock, the Little Brown Bat crawled away from him, then began to fly. She wound through the passageways of the mine toward light, but at the entrance she turned and fled inward. The band was strange upon her leg, but it was not painful. Soon she would no longer be aware of it, and might wear it without any harm for all of the possible twenty years of her life. If she was captured again or found dead, the band number would tell how far she had traveled or how long she had lived.

For a while after the man had left the cave, the Little Brown Bat remained awake. She captured and ate a number of mosquitoes. She drank from a small puddle of snow-melted water that had dripped through a hole in the tunnel ceiling. At last she pitched toward the ceiling and hung up close to a group of bats. She moved about restlessly, but finally she returned to the deep deathlike sleep of winter. The other bats that had been awakened by the activities of the man also returned to sleep. The silence of the long dark winter night returned.

SPRING

Near the beginning of April, the Little Brown Bat
began to awaken. An internal clock—the natural
time-sense within her—caused her to end hibernation. Again her heartbeat and breathing became
more rapid and her temperature quickly rose. At first
she was quarrelsome, yawned, and moved about. She
made a few short trial flights and returned to the
wall or ceiling. There for a while she remained
cleaning herself. She did this in the same way a cat
will wash its fur. With her tongue she licked the hair
while her thumbs smoothed, rubbed and helped with
the cleaning. She cleaned her ears and the area about
them for a very long time. These were very important
to her way of living.

The Little Brown Bat made several more trial
flights toward the sun-bright world beyond the cave,

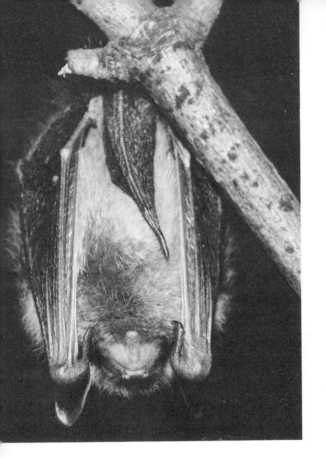
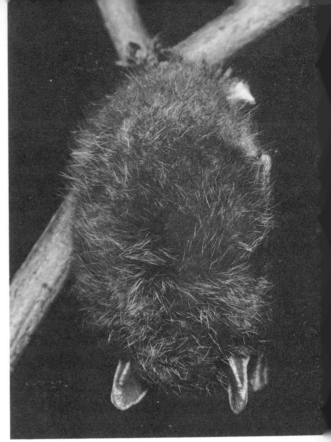

but each time she returned to rest. At dusk, she flew outward into the dimness. Her body was thin. The strong pangs of hunger filled her and drove her to hunt, but there were few insects flying in the cool early spring air. Her hunting flight carried her toward the small town below the mine. There were people moving about in the streets, but the Little Brown Bat gave them little notice. Near the glare of street lights were greater numbers of insects. There she hunted and fed for several hours, then hung from the branch of a tree and rested.

The night was half gone when again she began to fly. Her movements were no longer the random feeding flight of the earlier part of the night. There was a direction: a deep knowledge within her that moved her to travel away from her winter home and back toward the distant place from which she had come in the late fall. As the dawn light approached, she came upon a deserted farmhouse and slipped into the attic to hang upside down from the top beam.

The next night was very like the one that had just passed. She awoke at dusk and began to feed. She rested again, then continued her flight northward. For six more days she repeated this pattern of sleeping, eating, and movement, until she had reached the end place of her journey. One dawn she entered the open window of an old barn and flew to the upper beams to hang and clean herself.

There were many other bats within the building. Some rested while others flew about in the dimness and gave out shrill little cries or clicking sounds. Almost all of the bats remained clustered closely together near the roof beams, but a few crawled into

crevices between boards around the windows or in corners. All of these places gave the sleeping bats the things they found most comfortable: darkness and the warmth of the sun. For the next few months they would sleep in the barn all day and leave at dusk to hunt for insect food. At dawn they would again return.

All of the bats in the old barn were females, and their coming together to live was called a maternity colony. Within fifty to sixty days after awakening from the winter sleep, almost all would give birth to one or two babies.

Back in the mine, the male bats would continue hibernating for several more weeks. When they awoke they would leave the cave, but would not join the females until late summer or fall. Until then, they would live alone and seldom roost in the same place for more than a day or two. The temporary sleeping places would be many: the cracks and crevices of rocks, the holes of hollow trees, small openings behind house sidings or roof shingles, and under loosened bits of heavy bark.

SUMMER

It was the middle of June. All night the Little Brown Bat had hunted and fed upon the large numbers of insects that filled the air. Her body had lost its thin stretched look of early spring, and she was plump and healthy. Her soft brown coat glistened as she flew in the first pinkish light of dawn. She returned to the roost and hung herself on the roof beam as usual. For the next hour she carefully cleaned her fur with tongue and thumbs. At last she fell asleep.

There came into the barn on this day a boy and a girl that lived nearby. They had read of bats and the way the scientists study them, and wanted to try to observe for themselves. With a flashlight and notebook they entered the dimness of the loft and moved quietly so they would not disturb the bats. For many hours the children sat or walked about and watched the bats. They wrote in the notebook all of the things that they saw.

Shortly before noon the Little Brown Bat awoke again. It was hot in the loft, and the little creatures had spread apart from each other. For the next half hour she remained awake and seemed to grow more and more nervous. She moved about on the beam. She cleaned herself with quick jerky movements. She gave several little cries. At last she moved so that she no longer hung by her feet alone: her thumbs held to the beam as did her feet. Between the ankles of her legs and the tailbone, the thin dark membrane stretched to form a basket or cradle.

Within the body of the Little Brown Bat, a single baby had been growing. During the fall she had mated, but the growth of the baby had not begun until she had awakened in the spring. All winter as she slept, the sperm—or male cells—were held protected within her. When she awoke in the spring, the egg that had ripened was released from the ovary and moved into the thick elastic cavity of her body called the uterus. There it was joined by a single sperm and together they became the tiny beginning of a new bat.

Now in the early summer, the mother bat was in labor. The time had come for her baby to begin a life of its own. Soon it would be pushed out into the basket the Little Brown Bat had formed with her tail membrane over the end of her body. The muscles of her uterus began to contract or draw tight. She closed her eyes, bared her teeth and began to breath more rapidly.

The birth of the bat took only about fifteen minutes. For the last few weeks, it had rested crosswise within the body of its mother, but a short while before birth, it moved to a position head upward and feet down. As soon as its lower legs were free, it helped with its own birth by squirming and pushing against the body of its mother.

As the baby was born, the Little Brown Bat reached down to lick it clean. She also cleaned her own fur. The baby bat was followed by the still-attached afterbirth or placenta. This was the once liquid-filled membrane which had covered it, fed it, and given it oxygen while it grew within the mother. For several days the placenta would remain attached to the baby until at last the cord dried, broke, and dropped to the floor.

After a while the Little Brown Bat released one thumbhold from the beam and used her wing to turn the little one. With teeth and thumbs, the baby grasped tightly to its mother's fur, and moved along her body to one of the two nipples on her upper chest. There it would remain for many days to drink the warm sweet milk and to sleep. After a short time the mother bat returned to her normal way of hanging by her feet. One of the important happenings of her life was over for another year. She slept also.

Shortly after dusk, the Little Brown Bat left the deserted barn. The baby she had borne only a few hours before held onto her body with its teeth and claws. Throughout the long night it nursed or slept as the mother moved rapidly about in the darkness in search of insect food. At dawn the Little Brown Bat returned with her baby to the roost. She cleaned herself and her young one, then fell asleep.

In the barn there were many other mother bats with newborn young. Most of these had had a single baby, but a few had given birth to twins. Many of the young bats had been born on the same day, and many more had been born during the few days before or would be in the few days following. Most Little Brown Bats are born within the same short time period each year.

The children had watched the birth of the baby Little Brown Bat. Shortly afterward, they left the barn, but returned later with some friends. The baby bat was dry and sleeping. The children carefully removed it from the mother and placed upon its head a small dab of bright red fingernail polish. By this means they could tell it from the others and keep records of its growth.

At birth the little bat was already a fifth of its full size. There was only a sprinkling of hair upon its face and arms and legs. The trunk of its body was pinkish and almost transparent, but the muzzle, ears, wings, arms, and legs were dark. The ears had been bent forward over its eyes at birth, and would remain floppy for a few days. Its eyes were closed, and its head, feet, and thumbs seemed strangely large for the rest of the body. The tiny, sharp, back-pointing teeth were well developed and allowed the baby to clasp safely against its mother as she flew.

Each day the boy and girl returned to the loft and observed the baby bat. It grew rapidly upon its diet of rich mother's milk. On the second day its eyes opened, and a thick brown fuzz of hair had begun to appear on its body. Soon the young one had grown so heavy that the Little Brown Bat could no longer carry it as she fed. As she flew off to hunt each evening at dusk, she left the baby hanging in the roost. Each dawn she took it up again to clean and nurse.

When the children came to the loft at night they saw the baby hanging alone, and they were amazed by the ease with which it did so. Not all baby bats are so lucky however; some fall to the floor. Although the mother bats seem disturbed by the cries of the fallen babies, they do not pick them up, and the unfortunate young die.

Day after day the girl and the boy continued watching at the barn. When the Little Brown Bat was several weeks old they saw it begin to fly. At first it did not leave the loft of the old barn. Instead it flew in a circle that often stopped near the exit of the building, but it did not go outside. After a short rest, it would again begin its circled pathway within.

The flight of the young bat was very different from that of its mother. It moved with a slow steady beat, while grown bats most often fly in a fast zigzag pattern.

After three to four weeks, the young bat had reached its full size. The nail polish the children had

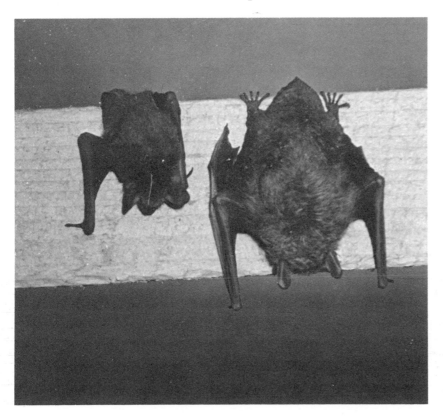

brushed on it had worn off and they could not tell it from the others. It no longer nursed from its mother and had begun to hunt for its own food. The mother Little Brown Bat did not show any special attachment for its baby. She was again as she had been before—a small furry creature hunting fast and alone in the night.

Late July. A moist warmth lay over the quiet rolling land, and the night was bright with the light of a full moon. The shapes of trees stood out black and sharp against the sky, and the small forms of darting, feeding bats could easily be seen. In midsummer, life was easy for the Little Brown Bats. Insects were everywhere. Mayflies, mosquitoes, black flies, moths, and gnats: all were plentiful in the night air. Early in the evening the Little Brown Bat had fed heartily and with ease, then she had rested and fed again. Long before dawn she returned to the barn and crawled under the siding of a window. She was warm and full. For a short while she cleaned herself, then fell asleep.

Another hour passed. From a distant farm there came the sounds of morning: the bark of a dog and the first shaky crowing of a rooster. Suddenly there was the high-pitched scream of a barn owl. Across the fields he flew, his large soft wings moving up and down with barely a sound. His head was turned downward so that his enormous brown eyes watched the hidden places of the earth. The owl was hungry. For him the night of hunting had been very poor; he had eaten nothing. The mice and other small animals that lived among the brush of the hills had remained carefully hidden from the bright light of the full moon. They had crouched in shadows and chewed upon the early seeds of weeds, or they remained underground nibbling the roots of plants.

As the owl winged his way toward his daytime roost in a deserted church tower several miles away, a bat zigzagged below him. The owl dropped downward, but missed his quickly moving target. He paused blinking upon the ground, then shook his feathers and again rose into the air.

A short while later, the owl turned from his pathway. He approached and entered the open window of the barn. There was a quick squeal, the fluttered

whisper of wings, and then silence. The owl flew from the barn window and landed in a nearby tree. From his claws dangled the body of a young bat. With slow but hungry motions he ripped away the flesh with his strong beak. The owl ate all parts of the bat. His body would solve for him the problem of what he could use and what he could not. Within the owl's stomach, the bones and hair of the bat would be gathered together to form a slender egg-shaped pellet. Several hours later it would be passed from his body. When the owl had finished eating, he was still hungry. He returned several times to capture bats and eat them in the nearby tree.

Under the board where she slept, the Little Brown Bat was unaware of the closeness of danger and death. Several times she jerked as though startled at the scream of a nearby bat, but she did not arouse or leave her hidden place. Some of the other bats had awakened and fluttered from the barn at the first entry of the owl. They flew around for a while, then returned to sleep. At last the owl went off to the deserted church steeple. Silence returned as the sun arose.

As the hour of sunset changed, so did the time at which most of the bats left the barn. Each evening as the light grew dim, the Little Brown Bat could be seen feeding over the same general bit of land. For so tiny an animal her movements were very fast. In a straight flight she traveled about ten miles per hour and her wings moved at the speed of fifteen strokes per second. Despite the speed at which she flew, her flight was perfectly controlled by the raising and lowering of her wings and tail. In this way she swerved, turned, and dodged in the air.

Suddenly the Little Brown Bat dove through the night air toward a large moth flying slowly between the space of two trees. The moth began to dodge and

turn away from her, but its attempts to escape were of no use. The Little Brown Bat netted it with a wing tip and knocked it into the basket membrane of her tail. Quickly she reached down and grasped the insect with her sharp small teeth. As she flew, she killed it, then while still flying, she chewed and ate the moth. When the Little Brown Bat had finished her meal, again she raced through the darkness. A second time she approached an insect: a mosquito. She captured it in her tail membrane without the use of a wing, again killed it quickly and ate. The use of her wing or her tail were the Little Brown Bat's most common ways of capturing food, but occasionally she simply grasped the insect directly in her teeth.

Despite the ease with which she captured food, the Little Brown Bat could see very little of the world about her. If she had been completely blinded it would not have changed her living very much. The Little Brown Bat had something that was of much more value to her than good eyesight. She had a bat's version of radar. As she skimmed about in the darkness, the Little Brown Bat uttered about twenty-five high-pitched clicking sounds every second. The sounds were so high that a person standing nearby

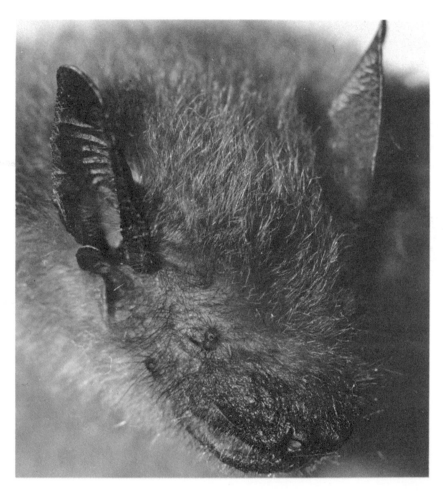

could not have heard them. The clicks were the Little
Brown Bat's system of echolocation: her way of find-
ing food or of flying by the echo of the sounds she

made. When the clicks hit something and bounced back to her, the Little Brown Bat could tell the location and size of the object she approached. If the echoes seemed to come from an insect, the Little Brown Bat lowered the pitch of her voice and clicked more rapidly. As she closed in on her prey, the cries became faster and faster until she was clicking two to three hundred times each second.

After the Little Brown Bat had fed for a while, she became thirsty. A small pond lay within her feeding territory. She quickly flew downward toward it, lowered her bottom jaw, and skimmed the surface. In this manner she picked up a droplet of water, then circled and repeated the same skimming movement eight or ten more times until she was no longer thirsty.

For many hours of the night, the Little Brown Bat flew, and before her she sent her high searching clicks. There were many insects to eat. For the Little Brown Bat, August was a time of plenty. It was a time of increasing health and a storing of fat for winter and hibernation.

A U T U M N

Slowly the year had changed. The hot dry days grew cold, and a sparkling white sheen frosted the world at night. The wild plants were in seed and the aspen trees had become brilliant golden rivers that marked the edge of dried-up streams. Dusk again came earlier in the evenings.

The Little Brown Bat was not really aware of the many differences about her. Season upon season flowed by and she only changed her behavior for the deep internal nudging—instinct—that controlled her life.

The Little Brown Bat awoke as the sun was setting. She yawned, stretched, and cleaned herself. About her other bats were awakening also, but there were fewer than there had been during the summer. Many of the older females had already left the barn roost

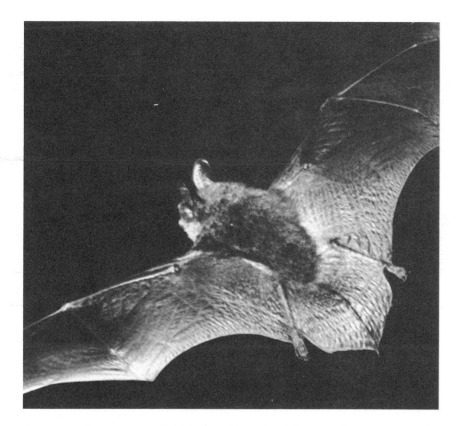

for another year. Their bodies had been fat and ready for the long winter sleep. The younger bats were still much thinner; they would stay awake and feed each night until at last the cold and the lack of food forced them to hibernation.

When the Little Brown Bat was fully awake, she

left the barn and flew low over the pond. There she darted and turned as she fed upon the many insects that had hatched from the water that night. Her sharp little teeth were busy crunching the crisp bodies of mayflies and mosquitoes, but in this the evening was unusual. It had been several days since she had fed so well.

There was in the Little Brown Bat a growing restlessness. At last it caused her to stop feeding and to swing over larger and larger areas of land. During the evening she came upon a male bat. Together they flew—first one after the other and then apart. It seemed a dance in the dark air. Before the night had finished, the Little Brown Bat had mated. During the following summer, again she would give birth.

Soon the Little Brown Bat began her flight southward. Within her the call had come. Her body was ready; there was a need for the long time of hibernation. Somewhere southward the hill waited and the dark cool mine that she had left in the early spring.

FACTS ABOUT BATS

Bats: creatures of the darkness, both furred and winged, and with faces uncomfortably human. From the earliest times people have wondered and told stories about these curious little animals. They have been called messengers of the devil and companions of witches, the souls of sleeping men, gods and the bringers of happiness.

The truth about bats is much simpler. These interesting creatures are mammals. They have hair, give birth to living babies and nurse their young, as do other mammals such as dogs, cats, rabbits, and man. But there is one obvious difference: the bat is the only mammal that can fly.

Millions of years before man first appeared on earth, bats were already diving about in the night sky. There were few animals that fed upon them, and even fewer that competed for the insects that flew in the dark. Bats flourished and spread over the earth. Some of those that were separated from each other gradually changed and could no longer breed together and produce living young. In this way there came to be many different species. Today they are found almost everywhere except in the cold treeless stretches of the far North and South.

The bats of the United States are all primarily insectivorous, or insect eating. They are very common and are divided into many species. All feed at night, fly by echolocation (the echo of high-pitched clicks), sleep hanging upside down, and in many other ways are very similar to the Little Brown Bat. The different kinds of bats differ from each other in many smaller ways such as size, the color of fur, the shape of the nose, and the length of the ears. All bats in cold climates hibernate, but those in the tropics do not. The temperature requirements for the place of hibernation—neither cold enough to freeze nor too warm—make caves an ideal spot.

Not all bats in the world eat insects. Fruit-eating bats are found in warm tropical regions where fruit is plentiful all year. They are very different from the small insectivorous bats of this country. Some are very large: the Flying Foxes may have a wingspan of almost five feet. Their eyes are large, the ears small, and they do not seem to use echolocation either to find food or to fly. Flower-feeding bats are also found in the warm tropics. They are small creatures with long pointed heads and brushlike tongues. They help to pollinate flowers in the same manner as do bees. Carnivorous bats eat other mammals. Fish-eating bats use echolocation and grasp fish at the water surface with strong, powerful claws. Vampires are small North and South American tropical bats that feed on the blood of large grazing animals. The bat makes a small cut in the skin of the sleeping animals and takes a little blood. The main danger of the bites is in the infection of the cut or in the passing on of rabies. A single bat does not take enough blood to weaken or kill the animal.

A lot of people fear bats, but with no good cause. Insectivorous bats have little interest in man, do no harm, and instead help us a good deal by eating large numbers of mosquitoes, gnats, flies, and other insects unpleasant to us. The droppings of bats—called guano—sometimes are mined and used as fertilizer.

Many people in the United States have made pets of bats and say they are quickly tamed and interesting to watch. They may be fed mealworms from a pair of tweezers. It is necessary to handle bats with gloves, however: a bite may pass on rabies.

If you want to study bats more closely, you may find them by looking in caves or in the attics of houses, barns, or deserted buildings of all kinds. There are several field guides of mammals that will help you to identify the types of bats you have found.

SOURCES OF PHOTOGRAPHS

Title page, pages 31, 34, 42: Leonard Lee Rue, National Audubon Society

Pages 5, 6, 10, 13, 14, 15, 16, 18, 24, 36, 38, 40: Rick Carron

Page 20: Donald S. Heintzelman, National Audubon Society

Page 22: National Audubon Society